Running

Jeff Savage

Crestwood House
Parsippany, New Jersey

Designer: Deborah Fillion
Photo credits—Cover: Jeff Savage
               Jeff Savage: pp. 1, 4, 10, 13, 16, 20, 31, 32, 35, 39, 44
               Runner's World: p. 7
               Bob Bentacourt: pp. 24, 25, 28
               John Zimmerman, AAF: p. 36
               Robert Hagedohm, AAF/LPI 1984: p. 42
               Wayland Publishers—Zefa: p. 23

Published by Crestwood House, an imprint of Silver Burdett Press.
A Simon & Schuster Company
299 Jefferson Road, Parsippany, NJ 07054

First Edition

Printed in the United States of America

10 9 8 7 6 5 4 3 2 1

Library of Congress Cataloging-in-Publication Data
Savage, Jeff, 1961–
    Running / by Jeff Savage.—1st ed.
       p. cm.— (Working out)
    Includes index.
    ISBN 0-89686-855-9   Pbk 0-382-24948-8
    1. Running. I. Title. II. Series.
    GV1061.S28 1995
    796.42—dc20   93-37943

Summary: A beginner's guide to running. Includes basic terminology, sample workout routines, expert advice, and a glossary of terms.

CONTENTS

Running can help you stay in shape and meet new friends.

CHAPTER 1

Becoming a Runner

Most of the boys in Amby Burfoot's seventh-grade class in Mystic, Connecticut, took off in a **sprint.** The race was 1 mile long, and the boys were elbowing one another to take the lead from the start. Not Amby. He kept a slow and steady **pace** that dropped him several hundred feet behind most of the other runners after one lap around the track. Amby realized that it took four laps to complete the race and that it didn't matter who was in the lead after one, two, or even three laps. What mattered to him was being the first one to finish all four laps.

At the end of the second lap, Amby was still behind a lot of the boys—but he was catching up. In the third lap, he began passing them. Whoosh. Whoosh. One by one, he strode past each boy until, by the start of the fourth lap, he was in front. And Amby never looked back. He coasted to the finish line well ahead of everyone else in his class. "I knew I wasn't a sprinter," Amby explained. "So I had to make it up with patience and **endurance**." Endurance is the body's ability to go on being physically active without running out of energy. At an early age, Amby had learned one of the secrets of running.

One year Amby got a summer job raking piles of seaweed on Main Beach in Groton Long Point, Connecticut. He would rake the slippery green plant into a big pile for a truck to haul away, then run a little way down the beach and start raking up another pile. He didn't care much for the raking, but he enjoyed the running. So much, in fact, that after he was through raking for the day, he would run a few miles on the sand, just for fun.

As a high school student, Amby joined the cross-country team and enjoyed running in all sorts of exciting places, like apple orchards. He also appreciated meeting new friends who seemed to enjoy running as much as he did.

Amby continued to run even after he grew up and became a schoolteacher in a sixth-grade class. "At the end of every day," Amby says, "my students would see me put on my jogging shorts and run home 12 miles."

In 1968, Amby Burfoot won the Boston Marathon. A **marathon** is a special race covering 26.2 miles. Marathons are held every year in New York City, Boston, and other places— including the Olympics. The Boston Marathon is one of the biggest races in the world, and Amby was never more proud than he was that day. Today Amby is the editor of *Runner's World,* which is the largest magazine in the nation for runners. Amby still loves running, and says all young people should run if they can.

"Kids should mix their running with other sports," Amby

Boston Marathon winner Amby Burfoot enjoys a healthy run every day.

advises. "Other fitness activities they can do are bicycling and aerobics. But they should understand that running is the simplest, purest form of fitness that there is. And it's fun."

Running was just as fun for Henley Gibble. For a while, at least. She was a tomboy growing up in Norfolk, Virginia, playing as many sports with boys as she could. She even won her school's 100-yard dash in sixth grade and got to compete in the stadium at the College of William and Mary. But when Henley got to Northside Junior High, she discovered there were no sports there that included girls. And that's when her running stopped. "I tried out for cheerleading, just like all the other girls," she says.

It wasn't until many years later that Henley began running again. Robin, her 12-year-old daughter, had won a 600-yard race at school, and Henley decided to help Robin train every day at a nearby track. One day, while Robin was practicing at the track, Henley decided to run, too, just as she did when she was a young girl. Henley started running around the track, and after only the first lap she was coughing and wheezing. She couldn't finish a mile without stopping to walk several times. Henley realized she was in poor condition and decided at that point to start running on a regular basis again.

Henley began running every day, and eventually she joined a group called the Road Runners Club of America. "The people in the club were really nice to me," Henley remembers. "They didn't laugh at me for being slow and gawky or wearing the wrong running clothes."

Today Henley Gibble is the executive director of the Road Runners Club, which has become the largest running organization in the world. There are more than 150,000 members in the Road Runners, and Henley is the group's leader.

"It's too bad there weren't sports for girls in school when I was growing up," Henley says. "But now there are plenty of sports for girls and it gives them a great opportunity to be active. All girls should take advantage of this."

Whether you already enjoy running, or you don't consider yourself much of a runner, you should know something about running: It's fun, and it pays off. If it seems as if everyone in your school is faster than you and it's too late to start running, consider what happened to a woman named Joan Benoit Samuelson. Joan didn't do much running growing up. She had fun like any other girl, but it wasn't until after playing field hockey in college that Joan decided to take running seriously. Soon she discovered that she was good at it. Joan qualified for the marathon in the 1984 Olympics—and she won the gold medal!

Kids of all ages find that running is an easy way to feel good and have fun.

CHAPTER 2

Why You Should Run

Almost anyone who can walk, can run. The question is, why don't teens run more often? Younger kids run around everywhere, but it seems that when boys and girls reach 12 or 13 years old, a lot of them begin to slow down. Some even think they're too cool to run. Why? One reason might be that running is so often used as punishment. Were you late to gym class? Run a lap! Didn't do your homework? Run a lap! Made a mistake at football practice? Run a lap! With teachers and coaches *forcing* children to run, they don't *want* to run. This is unfortunate.

Running can be rewarding in many ways.

Running is very good for your body. Your muscles grow stronger each time you run. Your lungs develop a greater capacity to hold oxygen. And the more you run, the easier it gets.

Running increases your endurance, and so you can be active longer without getting tired. As your endurance increases, your performance in other sports and activities will improve, too. In a

11

journal called the *Physician and Sportsmedicine,* Jack Wilmore wrote that running to improve endurance can help you in football. "Football is predominately a speed-and-power type of activity... however, when it comes time to play the fourth quarter, the endurance component becomes crucial. A player with poor endurance will be **fatigued** . . . and will be prone to more serious injury." Endurance obviously is important in other activities, like basketball, soccer, baseball, biking, and swimming.

A recent study examined the great physical and mental effects of running. A test group of sixth-grade children ran 30 minutes a day, three days a week, for four months. A control group of sixth graders stayed in the gym and participated in a regular physical education class. At the end of the four months, the group that ran was in much better physical condition than the control group, with stronger hearts, better **lung capacity**, and less **body fat**. And because they felt better and looked better, they had higher **self-esteem** (they felt better about themselves).

Running gets your heart beating faster and faster. According to the American Heart Association, it is important to exercise your heart at least three times a week, at least 20 minutes at a time, by getting it to beat almost twice as fast as normal. The hearts of young teenagers will beat about 90 times a minute. As teens grow older, the rate drops to about 80 beats per minute. In adults, the heart beats about 70 to 90 times a minute. Usually small hearts beat faster than big ones. This is true in animals, too. An elephant's heart beats only 25 times a minute. But a mouse's

A baseball player with strong endurance is likely to be a valuable team member.

heart beats 700 times a minute. When you get your heart to beat faster than normal by exercising, your heart will grow bigger and stronger. Just think of your heart as a muscle, because that's exactly what it is.

Running makes you feel good mentally. To be able to set a goal of running a certain distance and then achieve that goal is quite an accomplishment. It takes **discipline** and determination to be able to do it. You gain a great deal of satisfaction by showing yourself and everyone else that you have chosen a healthy way to stay in shape.

Running is inexpensive and can be done almost anywhere, at any time of the day. You don't have to buy a lot of fancy equipment—just sturdy shoes and comfortable clothing. And you don't need a track or a gym or any other special place to run—just a place that's safe (in the next chapter we'll talk about safe places to run).

Running is a great way to exercise with friends and to meet new people. You can run together in groups or with one other person and carry on a conversation as you go. Talking can help you maintain a slow, steady pace that lets you run longer distances.

Over time, you will feel more energetic and less tired by running. It sounds strange, but that's what happens when you increase your endurance. And when you run for 20 minutes or more, your body will produce hormones called **endorphins** that will make you feel good while you run and for several hours after you stop. The feeling is called the "runner's high," and it's natural and a lot better than messing with drugs.

After babies learn to take their first steps, they want to run. The desire to run is a natural feeling. There is an event at Duke University in North Carolina called the Run-to-Mom 20-Yard-Dash which is for infants from 6 to 13 months old. And the babies really go. Children have a desire to run, even as young as a year old.

As children grow up, some of them stay true to that desire. Many of them become great runners, and even compete in the Olympic Games. What if Carl Lewis and Jackie Joyner-Kersee had stopped running when they became teenagers because they thought they were too cool to run? They never would have won gold medals in the Olympics. But Lewis and Joyner-Kersee ran as kids and kept on running as adults. You can, too.

Unlike many other physical activities, running can be done almost anywhere. This boy is enjoying a barefoot run on the beach.

CHAPTER 3

Gearing Up

t would be fun if you could run barefoot. The trouble is, unless you can do all your running on sand at the beach, you'll be running on asphalt or dirt, and sometimes stepping on rocks, broken glass, wood, bugs, and everything else. So you need shoes.

There are shoes for nearly everything—dress shoes, high-top basketball shoes, tennis shoes, cowboy boots, sandals, and so on. What kind of shoes would be best for you? Well, you certainly don't need to spend a lot of money to get a good pair of running shoes. But you also don't want to run long distances regularly in just any old athletic shoe. One of the biggest mistakes beginning runners make is to wait to see if they enjoy running before getting running shoes. They start running in shoes that weren't designed for running, and the next thing they know, they've formed blisters that make them want to quit running altogether. Running shoes have special arch supports, heel construction, and soles that cushion your legs from the pounding. Get these! Shoes come in all sorts of brands and colors. The most expensive shoes, or the ones you see on TV commercials, aren't necessarily the right ones for you. When you go to a shoe store, try on several pairs and choose the pair that feels the most comfortable. Ask the salesperson for help in selecting the shoe that's best for you.

Now, what type of clothing should you wear? Smart runners follow one basic rule: They dress for comfort rather than for style. Because running has become so popular, fashion designers are always putting out new styles. But as soon as you buy the "coolest" outfit, another one comes along to take its place. Instead, you should wear clothing that keeps you comfortable. In the warmer months, wear loose-fitting, lightweight outfits. It's best to use cotton or nylon fabrics that won't trap heat, and lighter colors that deflect the sun. A sweatband or sun visor on your forehead is also a good idea. In colder weather, you should wear enough clothing to keep you warm—but not *too* warm. Remember, once you've been running (or doing other exercise) a few minutes, your **body temperature** rises automatically. You'll stay warm in temperatures above freezing (32°F) if you wear a sweatshirt and a windbreaker, and plain sweatpants. It's also a good idea to wear a warm hat, because more than half your body heat escapes through the top of your head. You can even run in the rain, as long as your body stays dry and you get into warm, dry clothes as soon as you finish your run.

The best runners are the smart runners. In the summer, smart runners run in the shade whenever possible. In the winter, they run in the middle of the day, when it's warmer. Smart runners stay safe by running with an adult or friend whenever possible. In fact, running together is a great way to motivate each other. Smart runners run on grass, dirt, sand, a sidewalk, a bike path, or a track.

They don't run in the street, where they may face the danger of traffic. Smart runners drink plenty of water before they begin. Severe loss of water can result in overheating or even **heat stroke**, especially for children. It's important to replace any water you may have sweated out of your body as soon as you can. It's even safe to drink small amounts of water as you run. Smart runners understand what to do when they get a **side stitch** (a sharp pain in the side): They take deep breaths through their nose and mouth and rub the area where it hurts. If the side stitch doesn't go away in a few minutes, they stop running. Side stitches are not usually dangerous. They are caused by many things, like eating or drinking too fast right before running. You should eat slowly all the time, but especially before you run. Above all, smart runners know to stop running if they get too tired or if they are hurt. There's always another day to run.

This girl is stretching her calf muscles before beginning her workout.

CHAPTER 4

Off and Running

Ready to run? Not so fast.

Before you go sprinting out the front door, it's important to take a few moments to warm up your muscles. This prepares you to get the most out of your running. Start by moving around. Do some **jumping jacks** or go outside and walk around or jog slowly. After three minutes or so, you're warmed up enough to stretch. If you stretch without first warming up, you may pull a muscle. Proper stretching gives your body **flexibility**, allowing it to move more freely, and it helps you run faster.

First, stretch your calf muscles (lower leg muscles). Stand at arm's length in front of a wall and place your hands on the wall. If a wall is not available, something sturdy will do. With your feet together, heels on the ground, and knees straight, bend your arms to lower yourself toward the wall. You will feel the pull in your calf muscles. Be careful not to go down too low or too fast—you may strain your back. Next, stretch your hamstrings (back of upper thighs) by standing with your feet close together and your legs straight. Bend forward slowly and try to touch your toes. Reach only as far as you can until you feel the stretch. Hold this position for several seconds. Next, stretch your groin (upper inner thighs) by putting the bottoms of your feet together and sitting like a frog. Then, stretch your left front thigh by standing on your right leg and pulling your left foot to the back of your left leg (lean against something for support). Now reverse the exercise to stretch your right thigh. Finally, stretch your upper body by lifting one shoulder up and then the other with your arms at your sides.

Cooling down is just as important as warming up. When you finish running, always walk or jog slowly for a few moments and then stretch the same way you did in your warm-up.

Everybody knows how to run, but there are a few things good runners do to get the maximum performance.

Good runners stay relaxed. They don't grit their teeth or clench their fists. They allow their bodies to fall into the rhythm of running.

Good runners run with their heads up and their bodies leaning forward just slightly (but not bent over). Elbows should be bent and arms should swing back and forth. Hint: The faster the arms swing, the faster the legs go.

Did you ever notice, when you watch track athletes in a race, that they don't gasp for air? That's because breathing while running is not the same as normal breathing. Good runners know to

This runner is cooling down by stretching her hamstrings.

Marathon races have become popular among all age groups.

breathe deeply from the bottom of their belly. And they breathe through *both* their nose and mouth at the same time.

You should run differently depending on whether you are going for speed or for distance. If you are running for speed, you should already be competent at distance running. After a good warm-up and stretch and a little light jogging, you are ready to practice sprints. Crouch down at a certain spot and say, "Go" in your mind. Then take off and run as fast as you possibly can for 100 yards or so. Remember, though, you should never push yourself harder than your body can go. Sprint running should be left for the more experienced runners.

Running for distance is much better for you physically than sprinting is, and most runners find it more rewarding as well. It takes a certain determination to be able to run a good distance over and over again. One of the first things good distance runners learn is pacing. Remember how Amby Burfoot (the Boston Marathon winner in the first chapter) used to win the mile races at school? Most of the other kids would take off at the speed of light in the four-lap race. Before they were halfway through, they were slowing down to a walk. Amby, who would start out slow and steady, would run right by them and win the race. Amby was pacing. He was regulating his speed at the beginning of the race so that he would have enough energy to sprint at the end, if necessary. In other words, he was saving some of his energy. The American Academy of Pediatrics says in a 1990 policy statement that it is safe for kids as young as 11 years old to run as much as 10 to 15 miles daily and even to compete in marathons (about 26 miles), as long as they are not overdoing it.

What is overdoing it? Let's ask the experts. Bill Bowerman, who wrote the book *Jogging,* says that a runner of any age should not start hard running until he or she can run for an hour without becoming overtired. For beginners, it's more important to learn to cover distance, no matter how slowly. In *The Aerobics Program for Total Well-Being,* Kenneth Cooper writes: "Research has shown that unless a person is training for marathons or other competitive events, it's best to limit running to around 12 to 15 miles per week. If you run more than 15 miles per week, you are running for something other than fitness and the emotional balance, good health, and good looks that accompany it."

Learning to be a distance runner may help you be a marathon winner one day!

CHAPTER 5

Making a Plan

Suppose your school was going to have a running competition in six weeks—and you wanted to participate. How
would you prepare? That depends on whether you are
already in good physical condition. Note: It is a good idea to get a
complete physical exam before beginning any type of exercise
program. Discuss your training schedule with your doctor to be
sure that it is right for you. He or she might suggest an alternate
plan that would be better for you. Here is a sample training schedule that may prepare you for a running event in six weeks.

Week 1: Walk or jog for 15 minutes (1 mile or less) three days,
such as Monday, Wednesday, and Friday. Go at a slow and steady
pace.

Week 2: Walk or jog for 20 minutes three days. See if you can
jog at least a quarter of a mile (one lap around most tracks) without stopping to walk. Continue your training at a slow and steady
pace.

Week 3: Walk or jog for 25 minutes three days. Try to jog at
least half a mile (two laps) without walking. You can pick up the
pace just a bit, but do not run fast.

Week 4: Jog for 30 minutes four days. Try to jog three laps without walking. If you feel strong while running, you can add some speed into your training. On each lap, sprint the first 100 yards or so. Be sure to slow down to a jog after 100 yards (about one quarter of a lap).

Week 5: Jog for 30 minutes four days. Jog 1 mile without stopping. If you're feeling strong enough at the end of the 30-minute jog, sprint 200 yards (half a lap) twice. Don't overdo it.

Week 6: You're probably ready to add more speed play into your workouts. Jog for 35 minutes four days. During each jog, sprint one lap (about 400 yards) when you feel strong and warmed up. Be sure to slow to a walk if you're feeling especially tired.

If you're going to use a training schedule, it's a good idea to keep a training log (diary). It will help you to keep track of your progress. Be sure to write down how far you ran, how much time it took you, how often you stopped to walk (if at all), and how you felt afterward.

Now you should be ready for the race. If it's a sprint competition, remember that you can go only as fast as your body will allow. Don't get discouraged. If it's a distance race, be sure to pace yourself. Good luck.

Don't expect to be a track star overnight. Building speed and endurance takes time and training.

Even if you've been a couch potato for years, it's not too late to start a sensible diet and exercise program.

CHAPTER 6

The Rule of Fun

You probably know that a lot of young people in this country are in poor shape. What does it mean to be in poor shape? An organization that is interested in helping young people get in shape—the American Alliance for Health, Physical Education, Recreation and Dance—published a list of ages at which kids should be able to run or walk a mile, and the time it should take them. They figured that girls between the ages of 9 and 12 should be able to go 1 mile in about 11 minutes. Girls age 13 and older should be able to make it in about 10 minutes, 30 seconds. Ten-year-old boys should be able to go 1 mile in approximately 9 minutes, 30 seconds, 11- and 12-year-old boys in about 9 minutes, 13-year-old boys in around 8 minutes, and 14-year-old boys in about 7 minutes, 45 seconds.

This is a good scale to use. But unless you already are in good enough shape to try it—don't follow it. Instead, make a goal of reaching your time in a few weeks from now; then start training (slowly!).

More important than times and records, though, is simply running. But such emphasis is placed in this country on winning, that everything else is often overlooked. As Amby Burfoot, the Boston Marathon winner, says, "When you run in a race with 30 people, one person is going to win and 29 are going to lose. It's no fun to lose." Unfortunately, he's right.

You don't have to join a competition to be a runner, though. There are dozens of ways that running can be noncompetitive and fun. Judy Young, the executive director of the organization that published the mile times for children, says she never cared much for the competition of a race. In fact, the first time Young entered a distance race, in Annapolis, Maryland, she was caught in the bathroom when she heard the starting gun go off. She ran out of the bathroom and tried to catch up with the other runners. Of course, Young didn't win that race. But she did feel good when she crossed the finish line—simply because she had finished. "It's not important to win the race," she says. "It's important to do your best." Young has some suggestions for kids who don't necessarily enjoy running. "Children who sometimes find running around a track boring could try running on a treadmill, where they can watch the minutes add up electronically," Young says. "Or they could run on the beach, or run with friends."

One running game you can play with a group is to find the distance on a map between your town and another town. Then add up the combined miles that your group runs each day and see how long it would take to get to that town. The St. Mary Medical Cen-

Try not to be too concerned with winning the race—just concentrate on doing your best and having fun.

ter in Long Beach, California, suggests using points of interest in determining distance. For instance, how many miles would it take to go from a school in southern California to Disneyland or Knott's Berry Farm? See how many days it would take your group to run that distance. If you're still looking for a little friendly competition but don't want the pressure of racing, you and your friends can each predict the time it will take each of you to run a certain distance. Whoever comes closest to their predicted time wins.

If you're a beginning runner, keep in mind that time is more important than distance. As long as you are jogging (or even walking) for at least 15 minutes, you are doing your body a favor.

Years of dedication and determination paid off for world-class runner Carl Lewis.

Some Expert Advice

Smart runners always try to improve their **stride**, their pace, their time, and everything else that has to do with proper running. They can do this by listening to advice from the pros. The Road Runners Club of America cares so much about children and running that it has provided these running tips from some of the greatest runners in the world. Here's what the pros say:

Alberto Salazar delighted running fans when he won the New York City Marathon in his first try, in 1980. He also set many records, including the American record for the 10,000-meter race. Take time to stretch, says Salazar. "Stretching can help reduce injuries and sore spots. By doing gentle, easy stretching about 10 minutes after running, you can keep your muscles loose and supple for your next run. It takes a little bit of extra time, but stretching will make your running safer and more enjoyable!"

Anne Audain, from New Zealand, won a gold medal in the

1982 Commonwealth Games in the 3,000-meter race, and later set a world record for the 5,000-meter race. Audain's suggestion is to have fun and be patient. "I could not run until the age of 14 due to bone deformities in both my feet, which required surgery at age 13. I was in plaster casts for six months and afterwards had to learn the correct way to walk and, ultimately, run. At age 17 I started to take running more seriously, and I went to the Olympics at 19. You may not be able to imagine competing for so many years, but at least keep this in mind: Take your time and be patient in improving. Enjoy your running!"

Don Kardong, a marathon runner from Spokane, Washington, is the president of the Association of Road Racing Athletes and has competed in the Olympics. According to Kardong, proper breathing is crucial to running well. "Kids often ask me whether they should breathe through their nose or mouth when they're running. The answer I give is that they should breathe through their nose *and* their mouth and, if possible, through their ears. When you exercise, you need all the air you can get. That doesn't mean you should gasp or gulp for air, though. Try to breathe deeply but smoothly. Keep your breathing relaxed!"

Henry Marsh from Bountiful, Utah, has set U.S. records in the steeplechase four times. The steeplechase is a 3,000-meter (almost 2-mile) track race that includes barriers and a water jump. Marsh has been on four Olympic teams. He says it's important to run in a steady, balanced way so your energy doesn't give out. "I've won many races by running my own pace while others ran too fast at

You'll probably find that your running workouts will improve your performance in other sports, such as basketball.

the start and then struggled to finish. Race at the speed you have prepared for in your training, even if kids around you are running faster. You'll find you'll run better, enjoy yourself more, and pass a lot of those other kids before you reach the finish line!"

Pat Porter is an expert distance runner who represented the United States in the 1984 and 1988 Olympics. Porter says that you don't have to run just on flat surfaces. "Running up hills is obviously more difficult than running on flat surfaces. But that's one reason why a hill workout can be a beneficial part of your running. Hill running strengthens muscles, which results in a more powerful and efficient stride. When you're running with your friends, it's fun to see who can be the first one to get to the top of a hill. But whether you're first or last, running up hills will help you run better on any **terrain**!"

Priscilla Welch, a great distance runner from England, surprised fans around the world when she set a new masters (over 40 years old) world record in the 1987 London Marathon. Watch out for traffic, warns Welch. "During my training runs, I see young runners taking risks while crossing roads. When they're tired or distracted, I know they're flirting with disaster. Young runners should remember to use proper crossings. If no crossings are available, make sure there is plenty of distance before passing in front of a moving vehicle. Try to be alert at all times when you're in traffic, and let's remember to be patient and respect the rights of motorists, just as we hope they'll respect ours!"

Kim Jones of Spokane, Washington, won the U.S. Women's

Marathon championship in 1986 and continues to set distance records. In order to run well, you need to eat well, Jones says. "When you run, you use a lot of energy. Since growing takes energy, too, it's very important to eat well. This means three good meals a day, combining vegetables, fruit, bread, and milk, and avoiding too much junk food, like potato chips, cookies, and ice cream. If you eat properly, you'll find you have all the energy needed for fast, strong, enjoyable running."

Lynn Jennings from New Hampshire was ranked as the number one American woman road racer of 1986, 1987, and 1988, and has competed in the Olympics. Jennings advice: Don't be afraid to run. "When I first started to run as a high school freshman on the boy's cross-country team, I had no idea of what lay ahead of me. But I thought, 'I can do it.' I considered myself a pioneer, someone who would cross wild frontiers to get to an uncertain destination. As a young runner, you may be doing something different than many of your friends, but there's nothing wrong with that. Getting in shape, testing your endurance, or running races takes confidence, much more so than simply staying with a crowd and not taking risks. Don't be afraid to try something different!"

Most Olympic runners stick to rigorous training schedules and health-ful diets.

Finding the Time

t's easy to come up with excuses for not running, and young people do it all the time. How many times have we heard these excuses?

"I'm too hungry."   *"I'm too full."*

"It's too hot."   *"It's too cold."*

"I don't have the time."   *"I'm too tired."*

"I'm busy with my friends."   *"I'd rather do..."*

It's very easy to find excuses, all right. But for every reason someone has for *not* running, there is a better reason *for* running. You've learned plenty of good reasons just by reading this book.

Millions of adults run all the time. Kids are now joining in the running movement. All these people wouldn't be running unless they enjoyed it. Hundreds of children arrive each year at San Diego State University to compete in the Special Olympics. These children are physically challenged (they have a disability), and some of them can barely walk, let alone run. But they do. And they enjoy it immensely. "People come to watch these children run, and I've never seen bigger smiles on faces than when these kids come running down the track," says Nancy Conroy, a coach for the Special Olympics. "The biggest smiles are on the faces of the kids themselves. These children don't think that running is hard. They enjoy it."

People naturally like to run. It's just that some of us have been conditioned to believe that running isn't fun or that it isn't cool. Well, now you know the truth. And the next time your coach or teacher tells you to "Run a lap!" you can say to that coach or teacher, "My pleasure!" and go off running with a smile.

People with disabilities enjoy the thrill of competition and the benefits of physical fitness through the Special Olympics.

To Find Out More About Running

BOOKS

Bowerman, William, and Freeman, William H. *High-Performance Training for Track and Field.* 1991. Leisure Press.

Fixx, James F. *The Complete Book of Running.* 1977. Random House.

Glover, Bob. *The Runner's Handbook.* 1985. Viking-Penguin.

Haas, Dr. Robert. *Eat to Win: The Sports Nutrition Bible.* 1985. NAL-Dutton.

Neff, Fred. *Running Is for Me.* 1980. Lerner Publications.

WHERE TO WRITE FOR INFORMATION

American Heart Association
    1615 Stemmons Freeway
    Dallas, TX 75207

IDEA: The International Association of Fitness Professionals
    6190 Cornerstone Court East, Suite 204
    San Diego, CA 92121-3773

President's Council on Physical Fitness and Sports
    Suite 250, 701 Pennsylvania Avenue NW
    Washington, DC 20004

Glossary

body fat The amount of fat as a percentage of total body weight.

body temperature The measured temperature inside the body. The temperature is influenced by exercise.

discipline The ability to focus on a goal and stay with it.

endorphins Hormones (chemicals) that the body produces as a result of extended exercise. The endorphins are carried by bodily fluids to different parts of the body.

endurance The degree to which a person can go without running out of energy.

fatigue Out of energy, or tired to the point of exhaustion.

flexibility The degree to which a body's muscles can stretch or move freely.

heat stroke Collapse or fever caused by exposure to excessive heat. Heat stroke results from lack of water.

jumping jacks A conventional exercise technique in which the exerciser jumps and lands with feet apart while clapping overhead.

lung capacity The amount of oxygen a person can process through his or her body.

marathon A long-distance running event that is 26.2 miles in length.

pace The speed at which a person travels. Ideally the pace is maintained for a specific distance. To pace yourself means to run at a speed you choose.

self-esteem Pride and confidence in oneself.

side stitch A sharp pain in the side experienced while running, and often caused by improper eating.

sprint Short distance covered by full-speed running, as opposed to slow, steady pacing.

stride The angle and distance taken with each step while walking or running.

terrain The type of ground cover, such as cement, dirt, sand, or grass.

Index